MW01224791

50

SHADES OF GREY PAPER

50 Shades of Grey Paper

ISBN-13:
978-1507642917

ISBN-10:
1507642911

Chris Green
ChrisGreen.com
Facebook.com/Chris

Cover design: Nathan Ruff, www.onenine.co

This book starts with one BLACK page and ends with one WHITE page. In-between are 50, (FIFTY!) shades of grey paper. NIFTY FIFTY!

We'll reference the Photoshop RGB (Red, Green, Blue) color system.

Using Photoshop, you get PURE BLACK when you completely remove all three colors (0, 0, 0). You get PURE WHITE when you mix fully saturated versions of all three colors together (255, 255, 255). You get a SHADE OF GREY (or GRAY) when you mix equal amounts of all three colors at percentages between 0 and 100 (or equal integers between 0 and 255).

The RGB color system conveniently gives 256 points of color (0 to 255).

0,0,0 for BLACK and 255, 255, 255 for WHITE.

That leaves 250 points in-between. Divided up by 50 shades means that each shade increased by an increment of 5.

Photoshop color pallet included with each shade for quick and easy reference! Six-digit Photoshop Hex Codes included as well!

COLOR: Is it GREY or GRAY?

According to Wikipedia:

GREY or GRAY is an intermediate color between black and white. It is a neutral or achromatic color, meaning literally that it is a color "without color."

The first recorded use of GREY as a color name in the English language was in AD 700. GREY is the dominant spelling in European and Commonwealth English, although GRAY remained in common usage in the UK until the second half of the 20th century. GRAY has been the preferred American spelling since approximately 1825, although GREY is an accepted variant.

http://en.wikipedia.org/wiki/Grey

Thank you to RapidTables for their online RGB to Hex color conversion tool:

http://www.rapidtables.com/convert/color/rgb-to-hex.htm
http://www.rapidtables.com/

This page on the right is 100% PURE BLACK.

The Photoshop RGB color code is 0, 0, 0.

The Photoshop Hex Code is: 000000

Enter red color (R):	0
Enter green color (G):	0
Enter blue color (B):	0

Convert | Reset

Hex color code (#):	000000
Color preview:	

The page on the right is shade of grey #1 of 50.

The Photoshop RGB color code is 5, 5, 5.

The Photoshop Hex Code is: 050505

Enter red color (R):	5
Enter green color (G):	5
Enter blue color (B):	5

Convert   Reset

Hex color code (#):	050505
Color preview:	

The page on the right is shade of grey #2 of 50.

The Photoshop RGB color code is 10, 10, 10.

The Photoshop Hex Code is: 0A0A0A

Enter red color (R):	10
Enter green color (G):	10
Enter blue color (B):	10
	Convert Reset
Hex color code (#):	0A0A0A
Color preview:	

The page on the right is shade of grey #3 of 50.

The Photoshop RGB color code is 15, 15, 15.

The Photoshop Hex Code is: 0F0F0F

Enter red color (R):	15	
Enter green color (G):	15	
Enter blue color (B):	15	
	Convert Reset	
Hex color code (#):	0F0F0F	
Color preview:		

The page on the right is shade of grey #4 of 50.

The Photoshop RGB color code is 20, 20, 20.

The Photoshop Hex Code is: 141414

Enter red color (R):	20	
Enter green color (G):	20	
Enter blue color (B):	20	
	Convert Reset	
Hex color code (#):	141414	
Color preview:		

The page on the right is shade of grey #5 of 50.

The Photoshop RGB color code is 25, 25, 25.

The Photoshop Hex Code is: 191919

Enter red color (R):	25	
Enter green color (G):	25	
Enter blue color (B):	25	
	Convert Reset	
Hex color code (#):	191919	
Color preview:		

The page on the right is shade of grey #6 of 50.

The Photoshop RGB color code is 30, 30, 30.

The Photoshop Hex Code is: 1E1E1E

Enter red color (R):	30	
Enter green color (G):	30	
Enter blue color (B):	30	
	Convert Reset	
Hex color code (#):	1E1E1E	
Color preview:		

The page on the right is shade of grey #7 of 50.

The Photoshop RGB color code is 35, 35, 35.

The Photoshop Hex Code is: 232323

Enter red color (R):	35
Enter green color (G):	35
Enter blue color (B):	35
	Convert Reset
Hex color code (#):	232323
Color preview:	

The page on the right is shade of grey #8 of 50.

The Photoshop RGB color code is 40, 40, 40.

The Photoshop Hex Code is: 282828

Enter red color (R):	40
Enter green color (G):	40
Enter blue color (B):	40
	Convert Reset
Hex color code (#):	282828
Color preview:	

The page on the right is shade of grey #9 of 50.

The Photoshop RGB color code is 45, 45, 45.

The Photoshop Hex Code is: 2D2D2D

Enter red color (R):	45	
Enter green color (G):	45	
Enter blue color (B):	45	
	Convert Reset	
Hex color code (#):	2D2D2D	
Color preview:		

The page on the right is shade of grey #10 of 50.

The Photoshop RGB color code is 50, 50, 50.

The Photoshop Hex Code is: 323232

Enter red color (R):	50	
Enter green color (G):	50	
Enter blue color (B):	50	
	Convert Reset	
Hex color code (#):	323232	
Color preview:		

The page on the right is shade of grey #11 of 50.

The Photoshop RGB color code is 55, 55, 55.

The Photoshop Hex Code is: 373737

Enter red color (R):	55	⌂
Enter green color (G):	55	⌂
Enter blue color (B):	55	⌂
	Convert Reset	
Hex color code (#):	373737	
Color preview:		

The page on the right is shade of grey #12 of 50.

The Photoshop RGB color code is 60, 60, 60.

The Photoshop Hex Code is: 3C3C3C

Enter red color (R):	60	
Enter green color (G):	60	
Enter blue color (B):	60	
	Convert Reset	
Hex color code (#):	3C3C3C	
Color preview:		

The page on the right is shade of grey #13 of 50.

The Photoshop RGB color code is 65, 65, 65.

The Photoshop Hex Code is: 414141

Enter red color (R):	65	
Enter green color (G):	65	
Enter blue color (B):	65	
	Convert Reset	
Hex color code (#):	414141	
Color preview:		

The page on the right is shade of grey #14 of 50.

The Photoshop RGB color code is 70, 70, 70.

The Photoshop Hex Code is: 464646

Enter red color (R):	70		
Enter green color (G):	70		
Enter blue color (B):	70		
	Convert Reset		
Hex color code (#):	464646		
Color preview:			

The page on the right is shade of grey #15 of 50.

The Photoshop RGB color code is 75, 75, 75.

The Photoshop Hex Code is: 4B4B4B

Enter red color (R):	75	
Enter green color (G):	75	
Enter blue color (B):	75	
	Convert Reset	
Hex color code (#):	4B4B4B	
Color preview:		

The page on the right is shade of grey #16 of 50.

The Photoshop RGB color code is 80, 80, 80.

The Photoshop Hex Code is: 505050

Enter red color (R):	80	
Enter green color (G):	80	
Enter blue color (B):	80	
	Convert Reset	
Hex color code (#):	505050	
Color preview:		

The page on the right is shade of grey #17 of 50.

The Photoshop RGB color code is 85, 85, 85.

The Photoshop Hex Code is: 555555

Enter red color (R):	85	
Enter green color (G):	85	
Enter blue color (B):	85	
	Convert Reset	
Hex color code (#):	555555	
Color preview:		

The page on the right is shade of grey #18 of 50.

The Photoshop RGB color code is 90, 90, 90.

The Photoshop Hex Code is: 5A5A5A

Enter red color (R): 90

Enter green color (G): 90

Enter blue color (B): 90

Convert   Reset

Hex color code (#): 5A5A5A

Color preview:

The page on the right is shade of grey #19 of 50.

The Photoshop RGB color code is 95, 95, 95.

The Photoshop Hex Code is: 5F5F5F

Enter red color (R):	95	
Enter green color (G):	95	
Enter blue color (B):	95	
	Convert Reset	
Hex color code (#):	5F5F5F	
Color preview:		

The page on the right is shade of grey #20 of 50.

The Photoshop RGB color code is 100, 100, 100.

The Photoshop Hex Code is: 646464

Enter red color (R):	100		⌂
Enter green color (G):	100		⌂
Enter blue color (B):	100		⌂
	Convert Reset		
Hex color code (#):	646464		
Color preview:			

The page on the right is shade of grey #21 of 50.

The Photoshop RGB color code is 105, 105, 105.

The Photoshop Hex Code is: 696969

Enter red color (R):	105	
Enter green color (G):	105	
Enter blue color (B):	105	
	Convert Reset	
Hex color code (#):	696969	
Color preview:		

The page on the right is shade of grey #22 of 50.

The Photoshop RGB color code is 110, 110, 110.

The Photoshop Hex Code is: 6E6E6E

Enter red color (R):	110	
Enter green color (G):	110	
Enter blue color (B):	110	
	Convert Reset	
Hex color code (#):	6E6E6E	
Color preview:		

The page on the right is shade of grey #23 of 50.

The Photoshop RGB color code is 115, 115, 115.

The Photoshop Hex Code is: 737373

Enter red color (R):	115	
Enter green color (G):	115	
Enter blue color (B):	115	
	Convert Reset	
Hex color code (#):	737373	
Color preview:		

The page on the right is shade of grey #24 of 50.

The Photoshop RGB color code is 120, 120, 120.

The Photoshop Hex Code is: 787878

Enter red color (R):	120
Enter green color (G):	120
Enter blue color (B):	120

Convert   Reset

Hex color code (#):	787878
Color preview:	

The page on the right is shade of grey #25 of 50.

The Photoshop RGB color code is 125, 125, 125.

The Photoshop Hex Code is: 7D7D7D

Enter red color (R):	125	
Enter green color (G):	125	
Enter blue color (B):	125	
	Convert Reset	
Hex color code (#):	7D7D7D	
Color preview:		

The page on the right is shade of grey #26 of 50.

The Photoshop RGB color code is 130, 130, 130.

The Photoshop Hex Code is: 828282

Enter red color (R):	130	
Enter green color (G):	130	
Enter blue color (B):	130	
	Convert Reset	
Hex color code (#):	828282	
Color preview:		

The page on the right is shade of grey #27 of 50.

The Photoshop RGB color code is 135, 135, 135.

The Photoshop Hex Code is: 878787

Enter red color (R):	135	
Enter green color (G):	135	
Enter blue color (B):	135	
	Convert Reset	
Hex color code (#):	878787	
Color preview:		

The page on the right is shade of grey #28 of 50.

The Photoshop RGB color code is 140, 140, 140.

The Photoshop Hex Code is: 8C8C8C

Enter red color (R):	140	⌂
Enter green color (G):	140	⌂
Enter blue color (B):	140	⌂
	Convert Reset	
Hex color code (#):	8C8C8C	
Color preview:		

The page on the right is shade of grey #29 of 50.

The Photoshop RGB color code is 145, 145, 145.

The Photoshop Hex Code is: 919191

Enter red color (R):	145
Enter green color (G):	145
Enter blue color (B):	145

Convert Reset

Hex color code (#):	919191
Color preview:	

The page on the right is shade of grey #30 of 50.

The Photoshop RGB color code is 150, 150, 150.

The Photoshop Hex Code is: 969696

Enter red color (R):	150
Enter green color (G):	150
Enter blue color (B):	150

Convert   Reset

Hex color code (#):	969696
Color preview:	

The page on the right is shade of grey #31 of 50.

The Photoshop RGB color code is 155, 155, 155.

The Photoshop Hex Code is: 9B9B9B

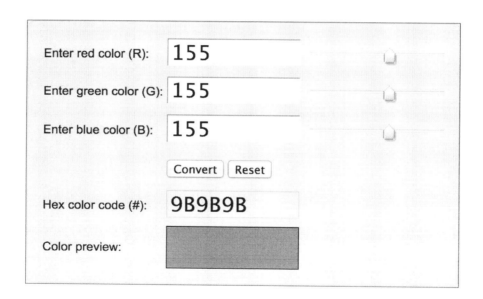

The page on the right is shade of grey #32 of 50.

The Photoshop RGB color code is 160, 160, 160.

The Photoshop Hex Code is: A0A0A0

Enter red color (R):	160	
Enter green color (G):	160	
Enter blue color (B):	160	
	Convert Reset	
Hex color code (#):	A0A0A0	
Color preview:		

The page on the right is shade of grey #33 of 50.

The Photoshop RGB color code is 165, 165, 165.

The Photoshop Hex Code is: A5A5A5

Enter red color (R):	165	
Enter green color (G):	165	
Enter blue color (B):	165	
	Convert Reset	
Hex color code (#):	A5A5A5	
Color preview:		

The page on the right is shade of grey #34 of 50.

The Photoshop RGB color code is 170, 170, 170.

The Photoshop Hex Code is: AAAAAA

Enter red color (R):	170	
Enter green color (G):	170	
Enter blue color (B):	170	
	Convert Reset	
Hex color code (#):	AAAAAA	
Color preview:		

The page on the right is shade of grey #35 of 50.

The Photoshop RGB color code is 175, 175, 175.

The Photoshop Hex Code is: AFAFAF

Enter red color (R):	175
Enter green color (G):	175
Enter blue color (B):	175

Convert   Reset

Hex color code (#):	AFAFAF
Color preview:	

The page on the right is shade of grey #36 of 50.

The Photoshop RGB color code is 180, 180, 180.

The Photoshop Hex Code is: B4B4B4

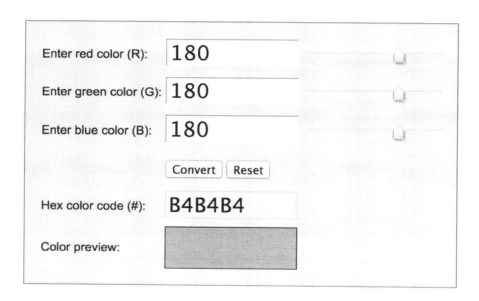

The page on the right is shade of grey #37 of 50.

The Photoshop RGB color code is 185, 185, 185.

The Photoshop Hex Code is: B9B9B9

Enter red color (R):	185
Enter green color (G):	185
Enter blue color (B):	185

Convert   Reset

Hex color code (#):   B9B9B9

Color preview:

The page on the right is shade of grey #38 of 50.

The Photoshop RGB color code is 190, 190, 190.

The Photoshop Hex Code is: BEBEBE

Enter red color (R):	190
Enter green color (G):	190
Enter blue color (B):	190
	Convert Reset
Hex color code (#):	BEBEBE
Color preview:	

The page on the right is shade of grey #39 of 50.

The Photoshop RGB color code is 195, 195, 195.

The Photoshop Hex Code is: C3C3C3

Enter red color (R):	195	
Enter green color (G):	195	
Enter blue color (B):	195	
	Convert Reset	
Hex color code (#):	C3C3C3	
Color preview:		

The page on the right is shade of grey #40 of 50.

The Photoshop RGB color code is 200, 200, 200.

The Photoshop Hex Code is: C8C8C8

Enter red color (R):	200
Enter green color (G):	200
Enter blue color (B):	200
	Convert Reset
Hex color code (#):	C8C8C8
Color preview:	

The page on the right is shade of grey #41 of 50.

The Photoshop RGB color code is 205, 205, 205.

The Photoshop Hex Code is: CDCDCD

Enter red color (R):	205
Enter green color (G):	205
Enter blue color (B):	205
	Convert Reset
Hex color code (#):	CDCDCD
Color preview:	

The page on the right is shade of grey #42 of 50.

The Photoshop RGB color code is 210, 210, 210.

The Photoshop Hex Code is: D2D2D2

Enter red color (R):	210	
Enter green color (G):	210	
Enter blue color (B):	210	
	Convert Reset	
Hex color code (#):	D2D2D2	
Color preview:		

The page on the right is shade of grey #43 of 50.

The Photoshop RGB color code is 215, 215, 215.

The Photoshop Hex Code is: D7D7D7

Enter red color (R):	215	
Enter green color (G):	215	
Enter blue color (B):	215	
	Convert Reset	
Hex color code (#):	D7D7D7	
Color preview:		

The page on the right is shade of grey #44 of 50.

The Photoshop RGB color code is 220, 220, 220.

The Photoshop Hex Code is: DCDCDC

Enter red color (R):	220	
Enter green color (G):	220	
Enter blue color (B):	220	
	Convert Reset	
Hex color code (#):	DCDCDC	
Color preview:		

The page on the right is shade of grey #45 of 50.

The Photoshop RGB color code is 225, 225, 225.

The Photoshop Hex Code is: E1E1E1

Enter red color (R): 225

Enter green color (G): 225

Enter blue color (B): 225

Convert | Reset

Hex color code (#): E1E1E1

Color preview:

The page on the right is shade of grey #46 of 50.

The Photoshop RGB color code is 230, 230, 230.

The Photoshop Hex Code is: E6E6E6

Enter red color (R): 230

Enter green color (G): 230

Enter blue color (B): 230

Convert   Reset

Hex color code (#):   E6E6E6

Color preview:

The page on the right is shade of grey #47 of 50.

The Photoshop RGB color code is 235, 235, 235.

The Photoshop Hex Code is: EBEBEB

Enter red color (R):	235
Enter green color (G):	235
Enter blue color (B):	235
	Convert Reset
Hex color code (#):	EBEBEB
Color preview:	

The page on the right is shade of grey #48 of 50.

The Photoshop RGB color code is 240, 240, 240.

The Photoshop Hex Code is: F0F0F0

Enter red color (R):	240
Enter green color (G):	240
Enter blue color (B):	240

Convert Reset

Hex color code (#):	F0F0F0
Color preview:	

The page on the right is shade of grey #49 of 50.

The Photoshop RGB color code is 245, 245, 245.

The Photoshop Hex Code is: F5F5F5

Enter red color (R):	245	
Enter green color (G):	245	
Enter blue color (B):	245	
	Convert	Reset
Hex color code (#):	F5F5F5	
Color preview:		

The page on the right is shade of grey #50 of 50.

The Photoshop RGB color code is 250, 250, 250.

The Photoshop Hex Code is: FAFAFA

Enter red color (R):	250	
Enter green color (G):	250	
Enter blue color (B):	250	
	Convert Reset	
Hex color code (#):	FAFAFA	
Color preview:		

This page on the right is 100% PURE WHITE.

The Photoshop RGB color code is 255, 255, 255.

The Photoshop Hex Code is: FFFFFF

Enter red color (R):	255	
Enter green color (G):	255	
Enter blue color (B):	255	
	Convert Reset	
Hex color code (#):	FFFFFF	
Color preview:		

There you have it!
50 shades of grey paper!

About the "author":

I'm just a dude with an idea so I made this book one night. I hope it made you laugh.

Want to connect?
Find me online at:

ChrisGreen.com &
Facebook.com/Chris

Made in the USA
Middletown, DE
21 January 2015